A Dog Came, Too

In memory of my godson A.F.B.J.,
another Alexander
— A.M.

For my mother
— A.B.

First United States Edition 1993

Margaret K. McElderry Books
Macmillan Publishing Company
866 Third Avenue
New York, NY 10022

Macmillan Publishing Company is part of the
Maxwell Communication Group of Companies.

First published 1992 by Douglas & McIntyre Ltd.,
Toronto, Canada.

Printed in Hong Kong

10 9 8 7 6 5 4 3 2 1

The text of this book is set in Plantin.
The illustrations are rendered in watercolor.

The illustrations of the friendly village are based on
reconstructions provided by Professor P. M. Hobler,
Simon Fraser University.

Library of Congress Catalog Card No: 91-44891
ISBN 0-689-50567-1

A Dog Came, Too

A TRUE STORY

BY Ainslie Manson
PICTURES BY Ann Blades

Margaret K. McElderry Books
New York

Maxwell Macmillan International
New York Oxford Singapore Sydney

Long, long ago, two native guides, an explorer, and seven voyageurs set off to find a route across Canada to the Pacific Ocean.

A big brown dog traveled with them.

He was not a pet. He was a working dog. All his life he had slept under the stars, not under a kitchen table.

He had never had his dinner served to him in a dog dish. He had never worn a collar or had a family to call his own.

The big brown dog didn't even have a name.

"Send Our Dog after him," the guides would say when they shot down a great white swan for food.

"Our Dog will swim and fetch it," six voyageurs would say when the seventh voyageur dropped his paddle into a swift-flowing river.

"Our Dog will keep watch," the explorer would say when there were bears or wolves near the campsite.

The explorer, the voyageurs, and the guides grew more and more fond of Our Dog as they traveled toward the Pacific Ocean.

IN that long, long-ago time, the land was still covered
with thick green forest. There were no roads to follow.
The rivers were the roads, and the men followed them all
the way across the vast land.

The explorer, the guides, and the voyageurs, plus all
their food, boxes, and bundles took up a lot of room in the
birchbark canoe. There was no space left for a big brown
dog.

Our Dog didn't mind. He liked to run along the shore and sniff out little animals. He chased chipmunks, squirrels, rabbits, groundhogs, and gophers. Once he chased a porcupine. He didn't do it again.

The big brown dog loved the guides and he loved the voyageurs, but most of all he loved the explorer.

Our Dog would come quickly from far away whenever he heard the explorer's whistle.

Our Dog would perk up his ears and listen whenever he heard the explorer's voice.

Our Dog could tell when the explorer was worried. He could tell when he was lonely, too, or sad or happy.

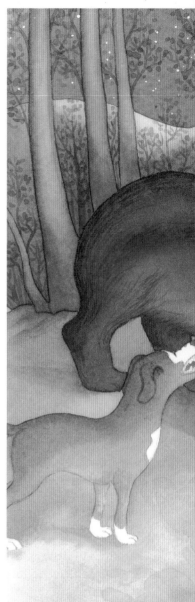

Each night, under the stars, Our Dog would lie down by the explorer's side.

Our Dog was a guard dog at night, and so he slept very lightly. He was aware of every sound in the deep, dark forest.

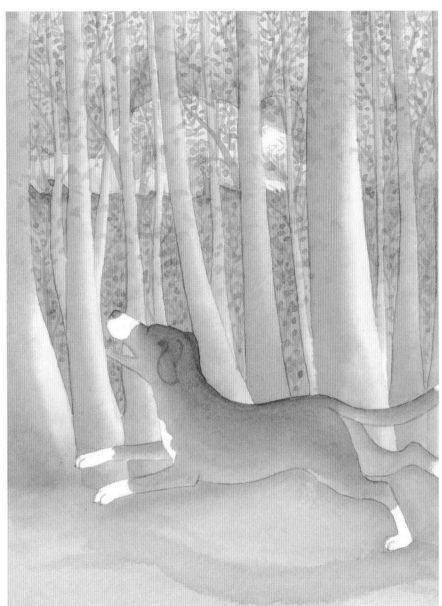

Once he saw a wolf prowling a little too close to the sleeping men. He barked to warn them.

Once he discovered a hungry bear trying to take their food. He chased it away.

Another time he growled to warn the explorer when a stranger crept by the campsite on his hands and knees.

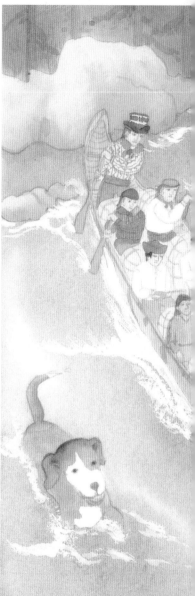

When the land was flat, Our Dog ran along the shore or on the open grasslands. He could always see the canoe, even from far away.

It was not as easy for the big brown dog when they reached the mountains. The canyons were deep and the rivers fast moving.

Sometimes Our Dog would swim along beside the speeding canoe, but the rapids were dangerous.

Sometimes he would run through the thick, dark forest high up the mountainside, and the canoe would shoot past him way down below.

I T was a long, long way to the Pacific Ocean. Our Dog grew very tired. His paws were cut by sharp, jagged rocks.

He was bitten by mosquitoes, wasps, blackflies, and fleas.

Sometimes there was little to eat, and there were no scraps for Our Dog. Tired and hungry, he would have to go hunting late at night for his meal.

The explorer, the voyageurs, and the native guides knew Our Dog was tired. They were tired, too. Often they had to carry their canoe and their boxes and bundles up one side of a mountain and down the other to avoid a dangerous rapid. They had little time or strength to sit by a warm fire removing burrs and twigs from Our Dog's tangled fur. They had little time or strength to look after their own comforts.

Then they came to a river that was worse than all the others. Our Dog could tell the explorer was worried. Time and time again they had to stop to repair the canoe. Eventually it was more patch than bark. It had become a patchwork canoe!

The men decided to leave that impossible river and travel overland to the ocean. New native guides they met in the mountains showed them a route that natives had traveled for hundreds of years.

After many days they reached a cool, beautiful valley. Our Dog noticed a different smell in the air. It was the smell of salt water. The sea could not be far away.

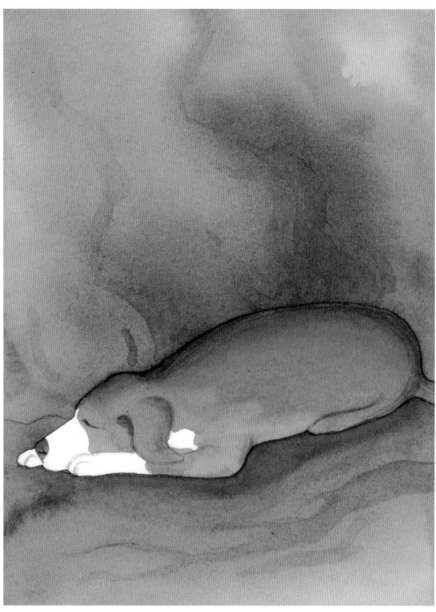

Before the last lap of their journey the men rested and were treated kindly at a friendly native village. They ate well and they slept well.

Our Dog knew his friends were safe in the village. He did not lie down at the explorer's side. He limped wearily off into the forest and found a deep, dark cave. He curled up and fell sound asleep.

OUR Dog slept too well. The next morning the men were ready and eager to go on to the Pacific Ocean.

The explorer whistled. For the first time ever, Our Dog did not come. He did not hear the whistle in his deep, dark cave.

The voyageurs called and called. Still Our Dog did not come.

The guides searched the nearby forest, but they didn't find him. In his deep, dark cave Our Dog was sleeping more soundly than he had ever slept in his whole life.

The men were sad and worried, but they had to go on. Joined by more guides from the friendly village and equipped with more canoes, they set off down the river on the last lap of their journey. Our Dog slept on.

When he finally awoke the next day, he trotted down the hill to the friendly village. Our Dog's friends were nowhere to be found.

He tried to follow their scent, but he could not follow it past the water's edge. He laid his head down upon his matted paws and stared at the river. He felt lost and lonely. He whimpered and whined.

When darkness came, he howled mournfully. Eventually the villagers could stand the noise no longer. They chased him away.

Our Dog knew the explorer usually followed rivers. So he, too, followed the river to the Pacific Ocean.

Where the river met the ocean, high mountains rose up into the clouds on either side of a long inlet. Our Dog caught the scent of his friends. They had camped here. But they had moved on. Now they were far down the inlet, well out of sight . . . and scent.

Again Our Dog laid his head down upon his matted paws. Again he whimpered and whined and howled. He was so sad and lonely that he stopped eating. He wandered up and down the river. He grew weaker and weaker.

The explorer, the voyageurs, and the guides had problems, too. Rain, fog, and high winds made travel dangerous.

One afternoon, when unfriendly natives surrounded their canoes, the men were forced to land on a small rocky point. The explorer, the voyageurs, and the guides spent a sleepless night. Our Dog was not with them to warn of further danger.

In the morning the men were alarmed to see that more and more unfriendly natives were landing on their rocky point. The voyageurs quickly packed up the canoes. But before they departed, the explorer painted a message on a rock. In years to come he hoped people would see his message and know he had truly reached the Pacific Ocean.

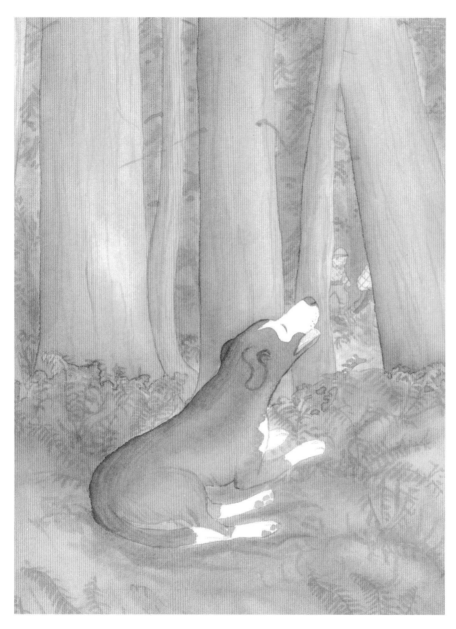

When Our Dog saw the explorer, the voyageurs, and the guides, who had returned up the river, he barked joyously.

Our Dog wagged his tail enthusiastically, but he was almost too weak and tired to stand up. The explorer knelt beside him, patted him gently, and whispered in his ear.

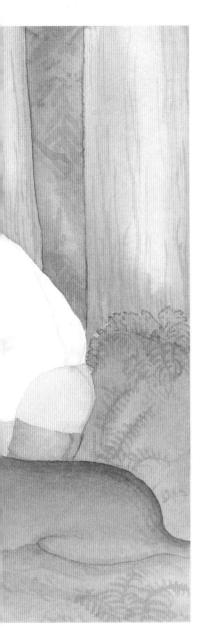

The voyageurs lifted Our Dog carefully and carried him to a canoe. Our Dog traveled as a passenger for the very first time.

With food and loving care, Our Dog recovered quickly. Soon he was well again and ready for the homeward journey all the way back across the vast country.

AFTER many weeks, as they neared the trading post that had been their starting point, Our Dog raced along the river's edge barking happily. The voyageurs began to paddle as fast as they could, while the explorer waved a big flag and the guides fired shots into the air.

They had traveled down rushing rivers and over snow-capped mountains. They had found the ocean they sought and they had returned safely. Now they prepared a huge feast to celebrate their journey. Our Dog sat by the fire with his nostrils twitching while his friends roasted a whole elk.

The guides allowed Our Dog to eat far more than his proper share of the tasty feast.

The voyageurs gave Our Dog seven hugs of thanks for all the help he had given them along the way.

And best of all, the explorer told him over and over again what a good dog he was.

The explorer, whose name was Alexander Mackenzie, kept a diary on the long journey to the Pacific Ocean. He wrote about all his travels and trials. He also wrote about the big brown dog, and that is how we know his story.

With the help of many native people along the way, Alexander Mackenzie became the first European to cross North America by land. He reached the Pacific Ocean on the twenty-second day of July, 1793. Our Dog was the first dog to make the long journey west.

DATE DUE		
NOV 1 4 1996		
RECEIVED NOV 0 7 1996		
JAN 0 6 1997		
RECEIVED DEC 1 2 1997		
MAY 1 2 1998 RECEIVED		
RECEIVED	MAR 2 9 1999	
MAY 2 1 1998		
JUN 0 8 1998	OCT 0 5 2002	
JUN 2 2 1998	JUN - 9 2006	
RECEIVED	RECEIVED	
2 2 1998		
MAR 3 0 1999	MAY 2 7 2006	